ARMED FORCES

★ ★ ★

UNITED STATES
MARINE
CORPS

by Jack David

BELLWETHER MEDIA ★ MINNEAPOLIS, MN

TM

This edition first published in 2008 by Bellwether Media.

No part of this publication may be reproduced in whole
or in part without written permission of the publisher.
For information regarding permission, write to Bellwether
Media Inc., Attention: Permissions Department,
Post Office Box 19349, Minneapolis, MN 55419-0349.

Library of Congress
David, Jack, 1968–
 United States Marine Corps / by Jack David.
  p. cm. — (Torque: Armed Forces)
 Includes bibliographical references and index.
 ISBN-13: 978-1-60014-164-5 (hbk. : alk. paper)
 ISBN-10: 1-60014-164-1 (hbk. : alk. paper)
  1. United States. Marine Corps—Juvenile literature.
 I. Title.
 VE23.D37 2008
 359.9′60973—dc22   2007042409

Text copyright ©2008 by Bellwether Media, Inc.

CONTENTS

★ ★ ★

Chapter One
WHAT IS THE UNITED STATES MARINE CORPS?   4

Chapter Two
VEHICLES, WEAPONS, AND TOOLS OF THE MARINE CORPS   8

Chapter Three
LIFE IN THE MARINE CORPS   17

Glossary   22
To Learn More   23
Index   24

★ ★ ★

The Marine Corps motto is *Semper Fidelis,* which means "always faithful" in Latin.

Chapter One

WHAT IS THE UNITED STATES MARINE CORPS?

The United States Marine Corps is known as one of the world's toughest fighting forces. Its soldiers are highly trained and disciplined. The Marine Corps is the smallest branch of the **United States Armed Forces.** The other branches are the Air Force, Army, Coast Guard, and Navy. The five branches work together to defend the nation.

The Marine Corps is an **amphibious** force. This means that its members can do battle on land and at sea. They work closely with the Navy. Navy ships carry Marines to places around the world. Navy ships drop off Marines on land to carry out **missions.**

There are no doctors or nurses in the U.S. Marine Corps. While on duty, Marines use doctors and nurses from the Navy.

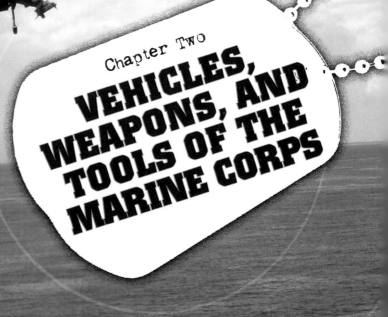

Chapter Two

VEHICLES, WEAPONS, AND TOOLS OF THE MARINE CORPS

AV-8 Harrier II

AH-1 Super Cobra

Like all branches of the military, the Marine Corps uses various vehicles to help them complete missions. Helicopters and aircraft help troops on the ground. The AH-1 Super Cobra is an attack helicopter. The AV-8 Harrier II is a strike fighter. They both use guns and **missiles** to destroy enemy targets and protect U.S. troops.

The AV-8 Harrier II can take off and land on very short airstrips. In fact, it can take off and land almost vertically.

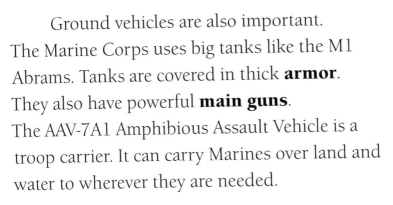

Ground vehicles are also important. The Marine Corps uses big tanks like the M1 Abrams. Tanks are covered in thick **armor**. They also have powerful **main guns**.
The AAV-7A1 Amphibious Assault Vehicle is a troop carrier. It can carry Marines over land and water to wherever they are needed.

AAV-7A1 Amphibious Assault Vehicle

The Marine Corps uses huge guns called howitzers. Howitzers can shoot ammunition more than 18 miles (30 kilometers)!

Howitzer

Every Marine learns how to use and maintain guns. The M16 assault rifle is the most common gun in the Marine Corps. Other guns include the Squad Automatic Weapon (SAW) and the M2 heavy machine gun. **Grenade** launchers and rocket launchers are explosive weapons used to hit large targets such as vehicles, airplanes, or buildings.

Rocket launcher

Machine gun

Marines use additional tools in carrying out their missions. They use radios to stay in touch with each other. Night-vision goggles (NVGs) help them see in the dark. **Camouflage** uniforms help them hide in almost any environment.

Night-vision goggles

Marines have conducted disaster relief operations in the United States and around the world. They have fought wildfires and distributed emergency food supplies. After Hurricane Katrina in 2005, Marines helped with search—and—rescue operations in Louisiana.

Chapter Three
LIFE IN THE MARINE CORPS

Intense training is required to become a Marine. Most members start with **basic training**. This includes classes and extremely difficult physical exercises. Everyone takes a test called **The Crucible** at the end of basic training. It lasts 54 hours. Students must work together to complete a series of challenges. When they pass, they are ready to be Marines.

New Marines are assigned posts at naval bases or on Navy ships. Every Marine has a **rank**. Most are **enlisted members**. This means they are under the leadership of **officers**.

Officers

Every branch of the U.S. Armed Forces has its own OCS. The Marine Corps OCS is in Quantico, Virginia.

Quantico, Virginia

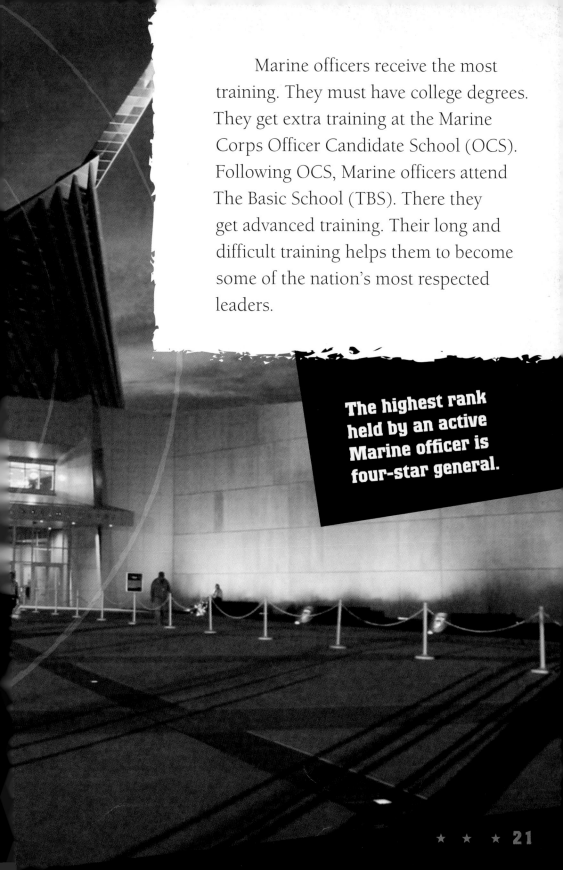

Marine officers receive the most training. They must have college degrees. They get extra training at the Marine Corps Officer Candidate School (OCS). Following OCS, Marine officers attend The Basic School (TBS). There they get advanced training. Their long and difficult training helps them to become some of the nation's most respected leaders.

The highest rank held by an active Marine officer is four-star general.

GLOSSARY

★ ★ ★

amphibious—able to function on land or in the water

armor—protective plating

basic training—the course of drills, physical tests, and military training that new enlisted members of the U.S. Armed Forces must go through

camouflage—made with patterns or colors that helps something or someone blend into an environment

Crucible, The—the intense, 54-hour test given to Marine recruits at the end of basic training

enlisted member—a person in the U.S. Armed Forces who ranks below an officer; all enlisted members are currently volunteers.

grenade—a small explosive designed to be thrown by hand or launched with a grenade launcher

main gun—the large gun on top of a tank

missile—an explosive that can be launched at targets on the ground or in the air

mission—a military task

officer—a member of a branch of the armed forces who ranks above enlisted members

rank—a specific position and level of responsibility in a group

United States Armed Forces—the five branches of the United States military; they are the Air Force, the Army, the Coast Guard, the Marine Corps, and the Navy.

TO LEARN MORE

★ ★ ★

AT THE LIBRARY

David, Jack. *United States Navy*. Minneapolis, Minn: Bellwether, 2008.

Doeden, Matt. *The U.S. Marine Corps*. Mankato, Minn.: Capstone, 2005.

Rustad, Martha H. *U.S. Marine Corps Combat Jets*. Mankato, Minn.: Capstone, 2007.

ON THE WEB

Learning more about the United States Marine Corps is as easy as 1, 2, 3.

1. Go to www.factsurfer.com

2. Enter "Marine Corps" into search box.

3. Click the "Surf" button and you will see a list of related web sites.

With factsurfer.com, finding more information is just a click away.

INDEX

★ ★ ★

2005, 16

AAV-7A1 Amphibious Assault
   Vehicle, 10
AH-1 Super Cobra, 9
armor, 10
AV-8 Harrier II, 9

Basic School, The, 21
basic training, 17

camouflage, 14
Crucible, The, 17

enlisted members, 18

four-star general, 21

grenade launcher, 13

howitzer, 12
Hurricane Katrina, 16

Louisiana, 16

M1 Abrams, 10
M2 heavy machine gun, 13
M16 assault rifle, 13
main gun, 10
missiles, 9
missions, 6, 9, 14
motto, 4

night-vision goggles, 14

Officer Candidate School, 20,
   21
officers, 18, 21

Quantico, Virginia, 20

radios, 14
rank, 18, 21
relief operations, 16
rocket launcher, 13

Squad Automatic Weapon, 13

United States, 16
United States Armed Forces,
   5, 20